Integrated Pollution Control:

A PRACTICAL GUIDE

Guidance issued by the Department of
the Environment and the Welsh Office

LONDON: HMSO

© Crown copyright 1993
Applications for reproduction should be made to HMSO
First published 1993
ISBN 0 11 752750 5

Contents

1 Introduction

1.1 This document provides guidance on the operation of Integrated Pollution Control (IPC) under Part I of the Environmental Protection Act 1990 ("the Act") and lists more detailed guidance which is available from various sources. It replaces 'Integrated Pollution Control: A Practical Guide', first issued in February 1991. IPC applies to the most potentially polluting or technologically complex industrial processes throughout England and Wales. The enforcing (and authorising) authority is Her Majesty's Inspectorate of Pollution (HMIP). IPC is being introduced progressively between 1 April 1991 and 1 November 1995.

1.2 A similar but separate system of IPC, also introduced by Part I of the Act, came into operation in Scotland from 1 April 1992, and will also be introduced in Northern Ireland.

1.3 Part I further provides the basis for a system for controlling emissions to air alone from generally less polluting processes. For such processes local authorities (districts and London and metropolitan boroughs, and in some cases port health authorities) are the enforcing authorities. Separate guidance relating to the local authority air pollution control system is available from the Department of the Environment (contact: 071.276.8322).

1.4 This Practical Guide, produced jointly by the Department of the Environment and the Welsh Office, explains the Act and the relevant Regulations made under it as they apply to IPC in England and Wales. All the guidance in this document is informal; it should not be taken as an authoritative interpretation of the Act nor of any subordinate legislation referred to in the document. It does **not** constitute guidance to the Chief Inspector pursuant to section 7(11) of the Act, although appropriate parts of it may be reflected in any such guidance.

1.5 Relevant information and guidance is also contained in:

(a) **The Environmental Protection Act 1990** itself (ISBN 0 10 544390 5, £14.45);

(b) **The Environmental Protection (Prescribed Processes and Substances) Regulations 1991** (SI 1991/472, ISBN 0 11 013472 9, £3.85), prescribing the processes and substances which come under HMIP and local authority control respectively and specifying the implementation timetable;

(c) **The Environmental Protection (Applications, Appeals and Registers) Regulations 1991** (SI 1991/507, ISBN 0 11 013507 5, £2.55), setting down the detailed procedures for the making and handling of applications and appeals and itemising the information which must be included in public registers;

(d) **The Disposal of Controlled Waste (Exceptions) Regulations 1991** (SI 1991/508, ISBN 0 11 013508 3, £1.00), providing for the interface between the controls under Part I of the Act and those under Part I of the Control of Pollution Act 1974;

(e) **The Environmental Protection (Authorisation of Processes) (Determination Periods) Order 1991** (SI 1991/513, ISBN 0 11 013513 X, £1.00), extending the standard 4-month decision period in certain cases;

(f) **The Environmental Protection (Amendment of Regulations) Regulations 1991** (SI 1991/836, ISBN 0 11 013836 8, £0.60), rectifying an inconsistency between SI 1991/472 and Schedule 15 to the Act, and correcting two minor errors in SI 1991/507;

(g) **The Environmental Protection (Prescribed Processes and Substances) (Amendment) Regulations 1991** (SI 1992/614, ISBN 0 11 023614 9, £1.05), clarifying one or two areas of uncertainty and correcting errors in SI 1991/472; and

(h) the **Chief Inspector's Guidance Notes** on specific processes, providing details of the processes covered in each Note, abatement equipment, the standards to be achieved and compliance requirements.

These items can all be obtained through HMSO. In addition, HMIP has produced the following documents which are available free of charge to applicants from HMIP offices:

(i) '**Application Form for an Authorisation under IPC and Guidance to Applicants for Authorisation**' – comprising a form for operators to use in seeking an authorisation and describing the sort of information HMIP needs to determine an application; and

(j) the **HMIP Integrated Pollution Control Fees and Charges Scheme (England and Wales) 1992.**

1.6   IPC is being applied to existing processes according to a rolling programme. It applied from 1 April 1991 for new processes of all descriptions and existing processes which are substantially varied, in addition to large combustion plant. **Annex A** shows the timetable set out in the Regulations (SI 1991/472) for bringing existing process categories within IPC. The process-specific guidance notes which the Chief Inspector is issuing to his Inspectors are being produced in advance of the dates on which the various descriptions of existing process come under the control of the system. Once published, these guidance notes will be available from HMSO.

2 Origins and Objectives of IPC

2.1 Releases of polluting substances from industrial processes to the three environmental media of air, water and land were subject traditionally to separate control regimes. However, the Fifth Report of the Royal Commission on Environmental Pollution (1976 —Cmnd 6371) proposed that polluting releases should be directed to the environmental medium where the least environmental damage would be done. This proposal was accompanied by the recommendation that a body be created with responsibility for ensuring that wastes were disposed so as to minimise effects in all three environmental media, thus achieving the optimum environmental solution overall. This is the basis of the term **Best Practicable Environmental Option (BPEO)** which is a key element of IPC.

2.2 These recommendations were reinforced in a scrutiny report on pollution control by the Cabinet Office Efficiency Unit in 1986. This reported that for as long as the three environmental media were treated separately there was a danger that the allocation of resources would not reflect an overall view of where the problems were most severe; and that the end result would be a haphazard disposal of pollutants unrelated to an overall assessment of the optimum solution for the environment as a whole. Accordingly, as a first step towards a new system of integrated pollution control in England and Wales, HMIP was established in April 1987. A consultation paper was issued in 1988, setting out the Government's proposals for a new system of integrated pollution control.

2.3 The main objectives of IPC are:

(a) to prevent or minimise the release of prescribed substances and to render harmless any such substances which are released; and

(b) to develop an approach to pollution control that considers releases from industrial processes to all media in the context of the effect on the environment as a whole.

It has the following additional aims:

(c) to improve the efficiency and effectiveness of pollution controls on industry;

(d) to streamline and strengthen the regulatory system, clarify the roles and responsibilities of HMIP, other regulatory authorities, and the firms they regulate;

(e) to contain the burden on industry, particularly by providing for a "one stop shop" on pollution control for the potentially most seriously polluting processes;

(f) to provide the appropriate framework to encourage cleaner technologies and the minimisation of waste;

(g) to maintain public confidence in the regulatory system through a clear and transparent system that is accessible and easy to understand and is clear and simple in operation;

(h) to provide a flexible framework that is capable of responding both to changing pollution abatement technology and to new knowledge on the effects of pollutants; and

(i) to provide a means to fulfil certain international obligations relating to environmental protection.

3 Prescribed Processes and Substances

Prescribed Processes

3.1   IPC applies to all processes in England and Wales falling within any description of process prescribed for the purpose by the Secretary of State in regulations. **The Environmental Protection (Prescribed Processes and Substances) Regulations 1991** (SI 1991/472, as amended by SI 1991/836 and SI 1992/614) list in Schedule 1 the descriptions of process to which the controls apply. The Schedule is divided into 'Part A' and 'Part B': 'Part A' processes are those prescribed for IPC; 'Part B' processes are those for local authority air pollution control. IPC regulates those processes with the greatest potential for serious pollution to the three environmental media; processes regulated under the local authority air pollution control system are those with less serious potential to pollute.

3.2   Regulation 4 excludes certain processes from control, even though they are listed in the Schedule. For example, exclusions may be appropriate if: prescribed substances are only released to air and land in quantities that are so trivial that the release cannot do any harm; processes are undertaken in a working museum; or the process involves the running of an engine to propel an aircraft or railway locomotive.

3.3   Schedule 2 clarifies what should be taken to form part of a prescribed process for the purpose of interpreting Schedule 1. Thus, in broad terms, once a process is defined in Schedule 1, all the related parts of the process come under control, provided that they are at the same location and carried on by the same person, and that they do not warrant authorisation in their own right.

3.4   The Regulations also contain the implementation timetable set out at **Annex A.** Schedule 3 to the Regulations sets out the transitional arrangements for existing processes, including the dates by which applications must be made.

Prescribed Substances

3.5   IPC is concerned with the control of releases to all three environmental media —air, water and land (as defined in section 1 of the Act). The Regulations list the substances which are most harmful or potentially polluting when released into the environment; these substances are subject to special requirements to ensure the use of the Best Available Techniques Not Entailing Excessive Cost (BATNEEC) to prevent their release to specified environmental media or (if that is not practicable) to minimise and render harmless such releases. All other substances which might cause harm if released into any medium are subject additionally to the use of BATNEEC to render them harmless.

3.6   There are three separate lists of prescribed substances according to whether the substance is to be controlled in relation to air, water or land releases. The lists of prescribed substances are in Schedules 4 (air), 5 (water) and 6 (land) to the Regulations; and are reproduced in **Annex B** to this guidance.

4   Application Procedures

The Application

4.1   **The Environmental Protection (Applications, Appeals and Registers) Regulations 1991** (SI 1991/507, as amended by SI 1991/836 and SI 1992/614) establish the detailed procedure for applications for IPC authorisations. The application must be made in writing and must contain the information specified in the Regulations. The details include: the name and address of the applicant; the address where the prescribed process will be carried on, with outline map or plan; a description of the prescribed process; a list of prescribed substances used in connection with or resulting from the process; a description of the techniques to be used to prevent or minimise releases; details of any proposed release of prescribed substances and an assessment of the environmental consequences; and proposals for monitoring releases.

4.2   The application also should point out clearly any information which the applicant wishes to be withheld from public registers on the grounds of national security or commercial confidentiality, as provided for in sections 21 and 22 of the Act.

4.3   Application forms together with further guidance on completion (see 1.5.i. above) are available from HMIP offices.

Timing of Applications

4.4   For *existing* processes—which form the vast majority of processes to come within IPC—applications should be made at the due time in the overall IPC implementation programme or when the process is to be changed substantially. For *new* processes with normal characteristics, and for which Chief Inspector's guidance exists, it will generally be appropriate for applications to be made when full designs have been drawn up, but prior to construction commencing.

4.5   For such processes which are not excessively complex or novel, it is likely that the operator will be in a position at the design stage to submit an application which provides all the information—including proposals covering management of the plant and training of operating staff—to enable HMIP to place it in the public register, carry out the required consultations and make a determination within the normal four month period. If, in the course of construction or commissioning, changes have to be made which would lead to the need for the authorisation to be varied, it would be open to the applicant to apply in the due way, or to HMIP to institute the appropriate variation procedures.

Staged Applications

4.6 For some novel and complex new processes, with long lead times for design and construction, it will not be possible for HMIP to determine an application at the design stage. It may be desirable in such cases for applicants to seek HMIP involvement at the earlier stage of process design, so that for example options relating to the best practicable environmental option are not closed off prematurely. In cases of this kind, the applicant should seek HMIP's agreement to the use of a staged application procedure, under which HMIP and the applicant agree a plan for the application and supporting information to be submitted in a number of tranches, as the process plans are developed progressively.

4.7 Once the use of the procedure has been agreed, it will be open to the operator to submit an application either at the point at which he is selecting the primary process, or—perhaps more commonly—when the outline of the process design is completed. He should provide as much information as he reasonably can at that time. The application will, subject to the normal rules on commercial confidentiality, be placed in the public register. It will need to be advertised by the operator and be subject to consultation in the usual way. However, by agreement between HMIP and the operator (under paragraph 5 of Schedule 1 to the Act), the application will not be determined within the usual four month period. Instead, under the phased plan, the operator will agree to provide HMIP with the additional information required to determine the application as it becomes available during the design, construction and commissioning stages. Each tranche of this additional information will, subject to the normal rules on commercial confidentiality, be placed in the public register and be subject to consultation in the usual way. At an appropriate point, usually at commissioning, the application will be finally determined. As the application will be open to public scrutiny and statutory consultation at each stage, possible objections to the proposal will be more likely to emerge at an early stage and the risks of significant abortive expenditure by the operator will be reduced correspondingly. Charges will be calculated for staged applications on the basis of time and resources required, rather than the usual application fee.

4.8 Even when the portfolio of Chief Inspector's guidance notes is complete, circumstances may arise exceptionally where an operator with a major and innovative new process or product in mind finds that no Chief Inspector's guidance exists, or the extant guidance is not directly relevant to the particular approach he wishes to adopt. It is for the operator himself to assemble the necessary expertise and information about available techniques to deliver the process or product, and HMIP will not provide free consultancy advice. However, in line with the transitional arrangements relating to the Chief Inspector's notes, HMIP Headquarters staff will be ready to consider with applicants the standards that are likely to be required. Approaches in such cases should be made to the Chief Inspector in the first instance. When the idea has been developed sufficiently, the operator should submit an application which may be handled through a phased authorisation procedure, as described above. At that time, HMIP may, if it considers it appropriate, place in the public register a record of any prior discussions that have taken place.

Additional Information

4.9 Paragraph 1(3) of Schedule 1 to the Act also gives HMIP the power to require the applicant to furnish any further information necessary to enable an application to be determined. However, there may be cases where it is necessary for HMIP to obtain information from other sources. Where it does so, the content of such information should be disclosed to the applicant and other interested parties and they should be given an opportunity to comment on it before the application is determined.

Time Limit for Considering an Application

4.10 Paragraphs 5(1) and (3) of Schedule 1 to the Act provide that the enforcing authority will have a set period in which to determine applications for authorisations. Where the application does not contain commercially confidential information or information affecting national security this will be four months from the date the enforcing authority receives the application. However, a separate Order under the Act—the **Environmental Protection (Authorisation of Processes) (Determination Periods) Order 1991** (SI 1991/513)—provides that where an applicant claims that the application contains details affecting commercial confidentiality or national security, the period will be four months from the day on which that claim is finally determined.

4.11 By agreement with the applicant, under paragraph 5 of Schedule 1 to the Act, HMIP may in appropriate cases take longer than four months to determine an application. This may be appropriate for design stage applications in particular.

4.12 **Figure I** shows the main steps and timetable for dealing with applications; **Figure II** sets out the procedures in more detail.

Refusal of an Application

4.13 HMIP must refuse to grant an authorisation unless it considers that the applicant will be able to carry on the process in compliance with the conditions to be included in the authorisation. Those conditions can only be set if HMIP has the information it needs. It is vital, therefore, that the application is a comprehensive document. If information is not provided in enough detail, HMIP will notify the applicant in writing of the additional information it requires and the time within which it should be provided. If this information is not forthcoming, HMIP then has the right under Schedule 1 to refuse to proceed with the application. The application must also be accompanied by the correct fee, otherwise the application will not be duly made and HMIP may refuse to consider it. Separate guidance which explains the fees and charges scheme under IPC is available from HMIP (see 1.5.j. above).

5 Consultation Procedures

5.1 Statutory consultees are identified in Regulation 4 of the **Environmental Protection (Applications, Appeals and Registers) Regulations 1991** (as amended), and include, for example, the Health and Safety Executive and National Rivers Authority. HMIP must notify them of an application for an authorisation, or a variation of an authorisation involving substantial change, within 14 days of receipt. The Act provides that statutory consultees will then have 28 days in which to respond. Where an operator has applied for information to be excluded on the grounds of commercial confidentiality or national security, Regulation 7 provides that this notification takes place not less than 14 days and not more than 28 days after the final determination of the application for exclusion.

Public Participation and Registers

5.2 The IPC system was designed to encourage a significant degree of public involvement in the decision-making process. In addition to an application being referred to specific statutory consultees, Regulation 5 provides that the public must also be afforded the opportunity to comment in respect of applications for authorisations, and variations of authorisations involving substantial change. The Regulation places a duty on the applicant to advertise in a local newspaper details of the prescribed process and its location, together with a statement that public representations may be made, and to whom.

5.3 The advertisement must be made not less than 14 days and not more than 42 days after the day on which an application for an authorisation (or variation) is made, or the day on which the holder of an authorisation is notified in accordance with section 10(5) of the Act. Regulation 7 again provides for slightly different arrangements for applications which contain commercially confidential or national security information.

5.4 HMIP must consider any representations it receives when determining the application. Before making representations, the public can examine the application, which must be placed in a register as soon as possible after it is received by HMIP.

5.5 In line with the Government's commitment to public access to environmental information, the Act provides for a system of public registers containing details of IPC applications and authorisations, of any variation or enforcement procedures, of monitoring information and of other relevant documents.

5.6 Registers of information on IPC processes are available for inspection free of charge at HMIP Regional Headquarters offices in Leeds, Bristol and Bedford and at local authority offices. Copies of entries may be obtained on payment of a charge. The registers at these offices hold information relating to IPC processes within their respective areas. In addition, an index to the entire register, but not the register itself, is available at HMIP Headquarters in London. Sections 20–22 of the Act deal with registers of information, and the exclusion from them of information on grounds of commercial confidentiality and national security information. Regulation 15 of the **Environmental Protection (Applications, Appeals and Registers) Regulations 1991** (as amended) provides more detail on the information that is contained in the register. A leaflet explaining the public's right of access to information under Part I of the Act —**'The Environmental Protection Act 1990, Part I AND YOU'**—is available free of charge from HMIP Regional Headquarters and from local authorities.

Exclusion on Grounds of Commercial Confidentiality

5.7 Section 22 of the Act allows for information to be withheld from the public register for reasons of commercial confidentiality, in circumstances where the disclosure of information would prejudice a person's commercial interests to an unreasonable degree. An applicant who seeks to have information kept or removed from the public register for reasons of commercial confidentiality should demonstrate that disclosure of the information would negate or diminish a commercial advantage, or produce or increase a commercial disadvantage which is unreasonable given the nature of the information and the financial effect of disclosure.

Exclusion on Grounds of National Security

5.8 Section 21 of the Act provides for information to be withheld from the public register when, in the opinion of the Secretary of State, its disclosure would prejudice national security. This provision is used only rarely, and may be initiated by either the operator or by the Secretary of State.

6 Authorisations

6.1 The Act (section 6) provides that no prescribed process may be operated after the date specified in the regulations for that description of process without an authorisation from HMIP.

6.2 HMIP is required to grant an authorisation, subject to any conditions which the Act requires or empowers it to impose, or to refuse it. HMIP must refuse it unless it considers that the applicant will be able to carry on the process in compliance with the conditions to be included in the authorisation. The Secretary of State has reserve powers to direct HMIP whether or not to grant an authorisation, and to make directions as to the conditions which are, or are not, to be included in an authorisation.

6.3 In setting the conditions within an authorisation, section 7 of the Environmental Protection Act 1990 places HMIP under a duty to ensure that certain objectives are met. The conditions should ensure that:

- the best available techniques not entailing excessive cost ("BATNEEC") are used to prevent or, if that is not practicable, to minimise the release of prescribed substances into the medium for which they are prescribed; and to render harmless both any prescribed substances which are released and any other substances which might cause harm if released into any environmental medium;

- releases do not cause, or contribute to, the breach of any direction given by the Secretary of State to implement European Community or international obligations relating to environmental protection, or any statutory environmental quality standards or objectives, or other statutory limits or requirements; and

- when a process is likely to involve releases into more than one medium (which will probably be the case in most processes prescribed for IPC), the best practicable environmental option ("BPEO") is achieved (i.e. the releases from the process are controlled through the use of BATNEEC so as to have the least effect on the environment as a whole).

6.4   The conditions in the authorisation must ensure that *all* these various objectives are met. If two separate objectives implied different standards (for example if one implied a tighter limit on a particular release than another) the tighter standard would prevail. In practice this means that HMIP must as a minimum ensure that BATNEEC is achieved, but may in some circumstances need to set more stringent conditions to achieve other section 7 objectives. An authorisation issued by HMIP will contain specific conditions to ensure that it fulfils the objectives contained in section 7 of the Act. Conditions may, among other matters, relate to the method of operation, the training of staff, abatement techniques used to reduce the release of substances etc. Releases will be regulated by conditions in authorisations limiting explicitly the substances that can be released to the various environmental media, and may be both in terms of their concentration and the amount of the substances released.

6.5   HMIP also has power to include any other conditions which appear to it to be appropriate. However, it would not be possible for HMIP to cover every eventuality in an authorisation. In addition, therefore, to the specific conditions required to be spelt out by HMIP in the authorisation, there is an implied condition in every authorisation that operators will use BATNEEC to prevent or, if that is not practicable, to minimise the release of prescribed substances into the medium for which they are prescribed, and to render harmless both any releases of prescribed substances which do occur, and any other releases. This implied condition complements the duty on HMIP to require the use of BATNEEC, and applies to all aspects of the process other than those regulated by a specific condition set by HMIP.

6.6   The implied condition is designed to cover the most detailed level of plant design and operation, where only the operator can reasonably be expected to know and understand what the demands of pollution control require in practice. For this reason, the Act provides that in any proceedings for an offence or failure to comply with the implied condition, the onus of proving that the operator was in fact using BATNEEC (and thus complying with the implied condition) falls on the operator himself.

Transfers of Authorisations

6.7 An authorisation for carrying on a prescribed process may be transferred by the holder to any other person. The Act requires the person to whom it is transferred to notify HMIP of that fact within twenty-one days of the transfer. Upon transfer the authorisation will continue to have effect as before subject to the same conditions. It is an offence to fail to notify HMIP of a transfer of an authorisation.

7   Required Standards and Best Available Techniques Not Entailing Excessive Cost (BATNEEC)

The Meaning of BATNEEC

7.1 All IPC processes under Part I of the Act are subject to the BATNEEC requirements. In general terms, what is BATNEEC for one process is likely to be BATNEEC for a comparable process. But in each case it is in practice for HMIP (subject to appeal to the Secretary of State) to decide what is BATNEEC for the individual process and the inspector concerned will take into account variable factors such as configuration, size, other individual characteristics of the process and local environment factors in doing so. Guidance on what constitutes BATNEEC for each description of prescribed process is provided in the Chief Inspector's Guidance Notes to assist both inspectors and operators.

7.2 It should always be borne in mind that BATNEEC is one of a number of objectives set out in section 7 of the Act, which must be achieved and in respect of which conditions will be included in an authorisation.

'BAT'

7.3 It is helpful to consider the words "best available techniques" separately and together.

7.4 'Best' must be taken to mean most effective in preventing, minimising or rendering harmless polluting releases. There may be more than one set of techniques that achieves comparable effectiveness—that is, there may be more than one set of 'best' techniques.

7.5 'Available' should be taken to mean procurable by the operator of the process in question. It does not imply that the technique has to be in general use, but it does require general accessibility. It includes a technique which has been developed (or proven) at pilot scale, provided this allows its implementation in the relevant industrial context with the necessary business confidence. It does not imply that sources outside the UK are 'unavailable'. Nor does it imply a competitive supply market. If there is a monopoly supplier the technique counts as being available provided that the operator can procure it.

7.6 'Techniques' is defined in section 7(10) of the Act. The term embraces both the plant in which the process is carried on and how the process is operated. It should be taken to mean the components of which it is made up and the manner in which they are connected together to make the whole. It also includes matters such as numbers and qualifications of staff, working methods, training and supervision and also the design, construction, lay-out and maintenance of buildings, and will affect the concept and design of the process.

'NEEC'

7.7 "Not entailing excessive cost" (NEEC) needs to be taken in two contexts, depending on whether it is applied to new processes or existing processes. Nevertheless, in all cases BAT can properly be modified by economic considerations where the costs of applying best available techniques would be excessive in relation to the nature of the industry and to the environmental protection to be achieved.

New Processes

7.8 In many cases, for new processes it is expected that BAT and BATNEEC will be synonymous. However, the following principles should apply:

- the cost of the best available techniques must be weighed against the environmental damage from the process; the greater the environmental damage, the greater the costs of BAT that can be required before costs are considered excessive;

- the objective is to prevent damaging releases or to reduce such releases so far as this can be done without imposing excessive costs; if after applying BATNEEC serious harm would still result, the application can be refused; and

- as objective an approach as possible to the consideration of what is BATNEEC is required. The concern is with what costs in general are excessive; the lack of profitability of a particular business should not affect the determination.

Existing Processes

7.9 In relation to existing processes, the Chief Inspector is concerned additionally with establishing timescales over which old processes will be upgraded to new standards, or as near to new standards as possible, or ultimately closed down.

7.10 Even though it relates to a single medium, the Secretary of State considers that the approach adopted in the EC Air Framework Directive is helpful in relation to the operation of IPC across all three media. Article 12 of the Directive, for example, which applies to all plants requiring an authorisation under the Directive, requires, where necessary, the imposition of appropriate conditions in authorisations, on the basis of developments as regards BAT and the environmental situation and also on the basis of the desirability of avoiding excessive costs for the plants in question, having regard to the economic circumstances of the industrial sector concerned.

7.11 Article 13, which applies only to processes existing prior to July 1987, requires certain factors to be taken into account:

"In the light of an examination of developments as regards best available technology and the environmental situation, the Member States shall implement policies and strategies, including appropriate measures, for the gradual adaption of [specified] existing plants to the best available technology, taking into account in particular:

- the plant's technical characteristics,

- its rate of utilization and length of its remaining life,

- the nature and volume of polluting emissions from it,

- the desirability of not entailing excessive costs for the plant concerned, having regard in particular to the economic situation of undertakings belonging to the category in question."

Release limits

7.12   Clearly BATNEEC may be expressed in technological terms, i.e. a requirement to employ specified hardware. It may also be expressed in terms of release standards. Having identified the best techniques and the releases they are capable of producing, it is possible to express BATNEEC as a performance standard: that is, a technique which produces release levels of X or better where X are the values yielded by the identified BATNEEC. HMIP will normally express BATNEEC in these terms so as not to constrain the development of cleaner techniques nor to restrict unduly operators' choice of means to achieve a given standard.

The Promulgation of BATNEEC

7.13   The inspector determining the case must decide what is BATNEEC in relation to each application, and translate that decision into conditions to be included in the authorisation. There must, however, be broad consistency in these decisions, especially between processes of the same kind. It is important for process operators and the public that BATNEEC is determined and applied in a transparent, rational and consistent way. In part this will be achieved by the application of the general guidance in the paragraphs above. A further important ingredient will be the guidance notes on each class of process which the Chief Inspector will issue to his inspectors.

The Role of The Chief Inspector's Guidance Notes

7.14   Process-specific guidance notes are being published in advance of the processes coming within IPC. These will be reviewed and updated if necessary at intervals of not more than four years.

7.15   These notes all have a similar structure. They:

- have an introduction which includes a definition of the process covered by the note;

- set out the general requirements for new and existing plant, including those of any plan or direction made by the Secretary of State; and

- set out the release limits to air, water and land which HMIP believes can be achieved by the application of BATNEEC and BPEO to the process.

Annexes then cover:

- a description of the process and the plant used;

- a list of the prescribed substances most likely to be present in releases to the environment;

- the techniques for pollution abatement which represent BATNEEC for the process;

- the monitoring necessary to demonstrate compliance with release limits; and

- additional requirements such as training and contingency planning.

7.16 In the case of new processes, it is expected that plant will be designed to achieve the standards in the appropriate guidance note. For existing processes, the guidance note will indicate the timescale on which it will generally be appropriate to upgrade to new plant standards. Inspectors will use these general standards as a backcloth in determining what is appropriate in each individual case, having regard also to variable factors, the sort of consideration listed in the Air Framework Directive and the need to achieve BPEO where there are releases to more than one environmental medium.

7.17 The standards included in the Chief Inspector's guidance notes are the subject of thorough review and consultation. Industry and other interested bodies have the opportunity to comment. The key stages in the process are as follows:

(a) review by HMIP or its consultants of best available techniques around the world. Techniques are identified which are used in or can be translated into a UK industrial context and which are or can be demonstrated to be commercially viable;

(b) before the first draft of a process guidance note is prepared, HMIP assembles an agenda of the key issues likely to be addressed in the note. This is circulated to those with a direct interest in the industry sector affected by the note, who thus have an early opportunity to comment on the proposed coverage and, if they wish, to suggest techniques and standards that should be considered;

(c) when a substantive draft has been prepared, HMIP circulates it for comment within Government and to the representatives of the industries and other bodies affected. The Chief Inspector takes the comments into account in preparing a further draft for wider, final consultation. If major questions about standards emerge, there may need to be fuller discussion;

(d) the guidance note is issued for final consultation within Government, with industry and with other interested parties; and

(e) following any changes arising from the comments received, the guidance note issues.

7.18 In this way, the Chief Inspector canvasses a broad spectrum of views in arriving at what he considers appropriate standards for each process. The Chief Inspector remains the final arbiter of what the notes contain, subject to any directions or statutory guidance from the Secretary of State.

7.19 Production of guidance notes to the timetable for implementing IPC requires that firm deadlines be set for each of the above stages.

Transitional Guidance for New Processes and Processes undergoing Substantial Change

7.20 Once a full portfolio of guidance notes has been established, there should be a clear and detailed framework within which operators can prepare applications. Some operators will, however, wish to submit applications in respect of new processes, or substantially changed existing processes, before the programme of developing guidance notes for processes is complete, or for processes which are so novel that published guidance for the process is not directly relevant.

7.21 In these cases, HMIP is ready to consider with potential applicants the standards that are likely to feature in future guidance, so that they can frame applications accordingly. Preliminary discussion of such standards is handled by HMIP Headquarters staff rather than by the local inspector, and correspondence should in the first instance be addressed to the Chief Inspector. This ensures consistency in areas where formal written guidance does not yet exist. The Chief Inspector may decide that it would be advisable to bring forward production of the appropriate guidance note.

Status of the Guidance Notes

7.22 The Chief Inspector's Guidance Notes have no statutory force. They do, however, represent the view of HMIP on appropriate techniques for particular processes and are therefore a material consideration to be taken into account in every case. HMIP must be prepared to give reasons for departing from the guidance in any particular case.

7.23 Where a guidance note exists, or guidance on standards is supplied for a particular case or purpose (as per paragraph 7.21), that guidance will not prejudice the final decision on a particular application, which will be taken following consideration of the applicant's case and of any representations from the public and the statutory consultees.

8 Variation Procedures

8.1 The Act enables either HMIP or an operator to initiate variation of an authorisation when a change to a process is proposed. Different procedures apply, depending on whether the change is "substantial" or "relevant".

8.2 HMIP's power, under section 10 of the Act, to vary an authorisation relates to an important aspect of the concept of BATNEEC: as pollution control techniques and technology improve or if the understanding of environmental risk changes, so the environmental standards required of industry should be changed. Section 4(9) places a duty on the Chief Inspector to keep abreast of developments in pollution abatement techniques and technology. HMIP has power to vary the conditions in an authorisation at any time, and it is under a duty to do so if at any time the conditions it then judges appropriate are different from those which the authorisation contains currently. The Act requires that the conditions in each authorisation shall, in any case, be reviewed at least every four years.

8.3 Section 11 of the Act provides for authorisations to be varied at the instigation of the operator. **The Environmental Protection (Applications, Appeals and Registers) Regulations 1991** (as amended) set out the procedure to be followed in this instance. The provisions are designed to cover a wide range of circumstances such as the upgrading and replacement of plant, the introduction of additional plant, the updating of control practices, changes in feedstocks, products, production levels or capacity, and so on.

8.4 Alternative procedures are provided to give the flexibility to cover the range of circumstances in which industry may need to seek variations. In the general case, where an operator wishes to carry out an alteration to the process, he can notify HMIP of the proposed relevant change, and ask it to determine whether the change would entail a variation in the conditions of the authorisation. If it would, HMIP must determine whether it would in fact consider making a variation, and if so what. The operator is free to consider in the light of that whether he wishes to continue with his planned change. A simplified procedure is also allowed for where it is clear from the outset either that what the operator wishes is a variation to the conditions themselves, as opposed to a change in the process which might entail such a variation, or that the operator is clear about the variation to the conditions which will be needed as a result of the proposed change.

8.5 It is not intended that IPC should handicap industry by imposing unnecessary delays or restrictions. Processes involving frequent changes in inputs, throughput and outputs, such as occur in the speciality chemicals industry, need to be able to operate within a regime that provides full environmental control but which allows the changes inherent in the process to take place without unnecessary delay. Under IPC it is possible in appropriate cases to define an "envelope" of release limits for the process in question, within which the operator is able to make adjustments without the prior approval of HMIP. The onus is on the operator to propose and justify such an "envelope" in his application.

Relevant change

8.6 A "relevant change" in a prescribed process is defined in section 11(11) of the Act as "a change in the manner of carrying on the process which is capable of altering the substances released from the process or of affecting the amount or any other characteristic of any substance so released". In practice, this is likely to embrace all but the most minor adjustments to the process and could include, for example, changes in the method of storing or possibly even the amount of feedstock stored on site.

Substantial change

8.7 There are arrangements for consultation and public participation if a proposed alteration is a substantial change. "Substantial change" is defined in section 10(7) of the Act as a "substantial change in the substances released from the process or in the amount of any other characteristic of any substance so released".

8.8 Guidance on what constitutes a substantial change for a particular class of process will be included in the relevant Chief Inspector's Guidance Note. Until a note covering a particular class of process is produced, a change will generally be regarded as substantial if it results in an increase in the rate, concentration or absolute quantity of a prescribed substance released, unless HMIP can be satisfied that no significant environmental harm will result. Where operators believe that a proposed change may lead to an increase in releases, they should consult HMIP Regional Headquarters in writing, who will determine whether or not the change is substantial.

8.9 **Figure III** of this guidance seeks to explain the key variation procedures diagrammatically.

9 Charging

9.1 The 1990 Act (section 8) provides for the Secretary of State to introduce charges to recover the costs incurred by HMIP in operating IPC. The charging scheme has now been set up, and covers the costs of considering and issuing authorisations, compliance monitoring, enforcement, sampling and analysis of releases, maintaining the public register, and associated administrative costs, but does not cover wider policy work.

9.2 The scheme operates on the basis of three categories of charges, as follows:

- an *application fee*, to cover the costs of considering each IPC application;

- a *subsistence charge*, payable annually, for the holding of each IPC authorisation, to cover the ongoing costs of inspection, monitoring and enforcement;

- a *substantial variation fee*, to cover the costs of considering an application for subsequent substantial variation of an authorisation.

9.3 In order to relate the size of IPC fees and charges to the amount of regulatory effort involved, payments due on a particular process will, in most cases, be linked to the number of defined "components" which the process contains, with the fees and charges under the scheme taking the form of flat-rate per-component sums.

9.4   Full details of the charging scheme are set out in the explanatory booklet which accompanies the IPC scheme (see 1.5.j. above). This lists the levels of charges for the three categories, and explains the circumstances in which each becomes payable, and any exceptions to the general rules governing charging. The method of payment is also explained, as are the consequences of non-payment.

10   Functions of HMIP

10.1   The Act sets out the various functions of HMIP with regard to IPC. The Secretary of State can also direct that HMIP should exercise the enforcement functions of a local authority specified in the direction as regards processes designated for local authority control. These transferred functions would relate, as do those of the local authorities, to the control of air pollution only. There has been little need to exercise this power to date.

10.2   Formally, most of the powers and duties referred to in this note as HMIP's are conferred on the Chief Inspector, who is appointed by the Secretary of State. The Chief Inspector has power to delegate any of his functions to other inspectors appointed by the Secretary of State for the purposes of IPC. The Act also confers a number of specific powers on inspectors—to enter premises, take samples, obtain information etc—to enable them to carry out their functions.

10.3   A list of addresses of all the HMIP offices is at **Annex C**, and a map of the areas covered by each is at **Annex D**.

11   Enforcement

11.1   HMIP has a number of powers in the Act to enforce the conditions of an authorisation. If HMIP believes that an operator is contravening any of the conditions (or is likely to) it may serve an 'enforcement notice' on him (under section 13). This will specify the matters constituting (or likely to constitute) the contravention and require specified steps to be taken, in a specified period, to remedy the situation.

11.2   Where HMIP considers that there is an imminent risk of serious pollution—whether or not there has been breach of the authorisation—it is under a duty to serve a 'prohibition notice' (section 14). The notice would specify the risk, the steps which must be taken to remove it and the time by which they must be taken. It would also suspend the authorisation for whatever aspects of the operation were causing the risk; and could in addition impose conditions relating to any part of the process for which the authorisation was not suspended.

11.3 HMIP also has power (under section 12) to revoke an authorisation by written notice. In particular, it may do so where it has reason to believe that the process for which the authorisation is in force has not been carried on for a period of twelve months. The Act does not, however, circumscribe the power: the Chief Inspector may decide, for example, to revoke an authorisation in cases where there has been persistent failure to comply with conditions.

11.4 In all these cases, the Secretary of State has a reserve power of direction over the Chief Inspector.

Offences and Remedies

11.5 The Act provides (section 23) that it is an offence, amongst other things, to operate a prescribed process without an authorisation, or in contravention of the conditions within an authorisation; to fail to give notice of a transfer of authorisation; to fail to comply with an enforcement or prohibition notice; to fail (without reasonable excuse) to comply with a requirement imposed by an inspector under his powers of entry, or intentionally to obstruct him in exercising those powers; ,to fail (without reasonable excuse) to comply with a requirement to provide information, or knowingly or recklessly to make a false or misleading statement; and intentionally to make a false entry in any record required to be kept as a condition of authorisation.

11.6 As an alternative to prosecution in the Magistrates' Court for alleged failure to comply with an enforcement or prohibition notice, HMIP may, in order to secure compliance with the notice, take proceedings against the operator in the High Court (section 24).

11.7 A court may, by virtue of section 26, instead of or as well as imposing a penalty for breaching an authorisation or prohibition or enforcement notice, order the person convicted of the offence to take specified steps that are within his power to remedy the matters that were the subject of the offence. The order may also specify the time within which the steps must be taken. In addition, the Chief Inspector, with the approval of the Secretary of State, is empowered to arrange for reasonable steps to be taken to remedy any harm caused as the result of such an offence. The operator may be required to pay the full costs of such clean-up action (section 27).

11.8 General provisions of the Act provide that, where an offence committed by a body corporate is proved to have been committed with the consent or connivance of or because of the neglect of any director, manager or similar officer of the body, that officer is liable as well as the body corporate itself.

Crown Immunity

11.9 Under the Act, IPC processes operated by the Crown are subject to control by HMIP in the normal way. HMIP is able to set conditions in authorisations and to issue other notices. Information on IPC processes operated by the Crown are, subject to any exclusion for reasons of national security or commercial confidentiality, placed in the public register. If breaches of authorisations occur in Crown run premises, it is not possible for HMIP to institute criminal proceedings; but HMIP is able, under section 159 of the Act, to apply to the High Court for a declaration that such a breach is unlawful.

12 Appeals

12.1 The Act gives operators a right of appeal to the Secretary of State against:

- the refusal to grant or vary an authorisation; the revocation of an authorisation; the conditions attached to an authorisation; variation, enforcement and prohibition notices (section 15 of the Act); or

- a determination that information is not commercially confidential, and must as a consequence be included in the public register (section 22(5) of the Act).

12.2 An appeal against revocation has the effect of suspending that revocation, but appeals against other notices do not have this effect. An appeal against a determination that information is not commercially confidential has the effect of preventing the entry of the information in the register pending the final determination or withdrawal of the appeal.

12.3 The appeals system is given effect by the **Environmental Protection (Applications, Appeals and Registers) Regulations 1991** (as amended). Regulation 9 requires that any appeal must be made in writing to the Secretary of State, and must be accompanied by the documents specified in the Regulations. Appeals should be addressed to the Secretary of State, and sent to the Department of the Environment, IPC Appeals Branch, Room AGO1, Romney House, 43 Marsham Street, London SW1P 3PY (for sites in England); or to the Welsh Office, IPC Appeals, Environment Division 3, Cathays Park, Cardiff CF1 3NQ (for sites in Wales). In section 15 cases, HMIP will place the notice of appeal in the public register.

12.4 The Regulations also specify in Regulation 10 the time limits for bringing an appeal: for section 15 appeals (except for appeals against revocation) these deadlines may be extended by the Secretary of State, but he would consider doing so only in the most compelling circumstances. If the appeal is out of time, and no extension is allowed, the appeal will not be considered.

12.5 The appellant must state, when making the appeal, whether written representations or a hearing is the desired method of proceeding. A hearing will be held if either party asks for it, or if, exceptionally, the Secretary of State determines that a hearing is the more appropriate course.

12.6 A notice specifying the date, time and place for the holding of a hearing of a section 15 appeal must normally be published in the locality of the process, and will be sent to persons who have made representations about the appeal. The procedure at a hearing is left to the appeal inspector, but he will be concerned to ensure that interested parties who wish to give evidence have a fair opportunity to do so.

12.7 The written representations procedure is explained diagrammatically in **Figure IV.** The procedures adopted by the Department on receipt of an appeal, whether dealt with by written representations or following a hearing, are specified in the Regulations. More detailed guidance will be available from the Department in due course.

13   Interface with other Legislation

13.1 The essential feature of IPC is that releases to all three environmental media are controlled by a single authority at one and the same time and BATNEEC is applied to the process which produces them in order to minimise the total environmental impact. As well as the environmental benefits of this approach, there are important practical benefits to all parties, not least that of "one stop shopping" for operators, who need deal as a result with only one enforcing authority for the process.

13.2 In recognition of its role in ensuring quality standards for controlled waters, the **National Rivers Authority (NRA)** is consulted by HMIP about all applications relating to processes which involve releases into such waters. The NRA has the power to require HMIP to set conditions within its authorisation relating to discharges to controlled waters (although HMIP may set additional or tighter conditions over releases to water, if for example higher standards are available under BATNEEC than those required by the NRA to safeguard water quality objectives). If the NRA certifies that in its opinion a release will lead to a failure to achieve a water quality objective, the authorisation cannot be granted. The NRA has powers to require HMIP to vary the conditions of an authorisation at any time. Its monitoring functions as regards the water environment and its powers to take proceedings are unaffected by these arrangements. A Memorandum of Understanding sets out the agreement between HMIP and the NRA on their respective roles and the working relationship between them. Copies are available from HMIP's London Headquarters.

13.3 HMIP is empowered to set conditions relating to the *generation and management* of wastes, whether intended for recycling, incineration, landfill or any other treatment or disposal. But IPC does not cover the final disposal of wastes in or on land. Such operations remain subject to separate control by the **Waste Regulation Authority**

(WRA), and no conditions in the IPC authorisation will regulate it. HMIP is obliged to inform the WRA when waste generated from a process will require landfill disposal.

13.4   IPC is not designed to cover the keeping, use or disposal of radioactive substances, which are the subject of the **Radioactive Substances Act 1960 (RSA 60)**. Because of the very distinct nature of these substances, an IPC process involving the keeping, use or disposal of radioactive substances will continue to require registration or authorisation under that Act. If conflicting terms were placed on an operator by HMIP under section 7 of the Act and by a regulation or authorisation under the RSA 60, then the "IPC conditions" would not apply.

13.5   The objective of the authorisations issued under Part I of the Act is to achieve environmental, not worker, protection (see section 7(1) of the Act). Full co-operation between the **Health and Safety Executive (HSE)** and their agents on the one hand and HMIP inspectors on the other is important to ensure that the controls that each place on scheduled processes are effective and compatible. Neither set of controls should affect adversely the protection of the environment or of workers. Where environmental protection demands tighter standards of control than are required to safeguard persons at work, these tighter standards should apply provided that they have no adverse effects on worker protection. HSE are consulted in advance on the guidance notes that are produced specifying the appropriate controls for particular industrial sectors before issue, and any general conflicts that can be anticipated are resolved. They are also statutory consultees on individual applications. Copies of the Memorandum of Understanding between HMIP and HSE are available from HMIP's London Headquarters.

Figure I: Applications —main steps and timetable

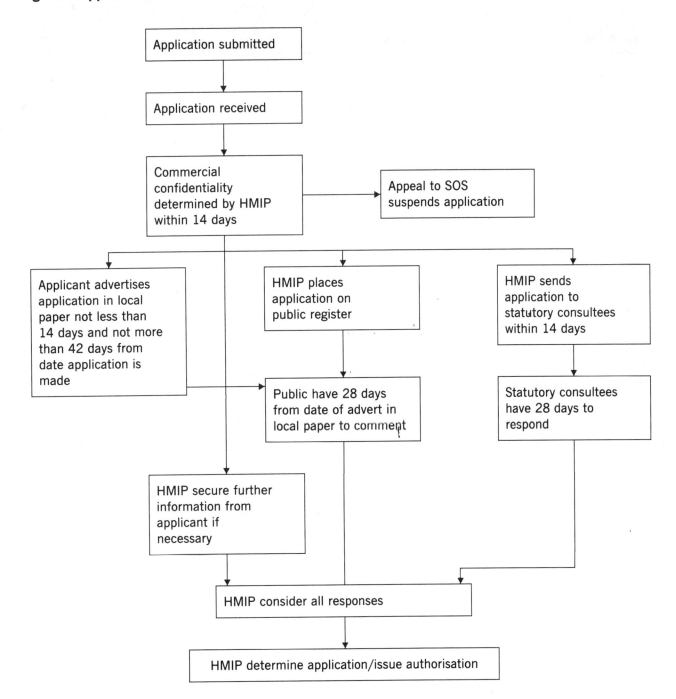

Figure II: Applications —detailed procedures

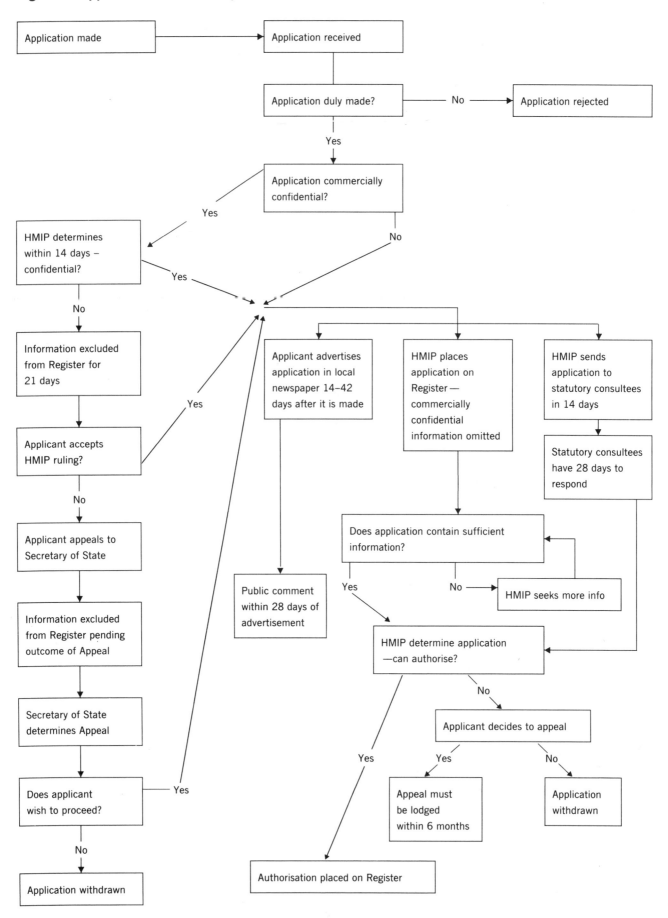

Figure III: Variations

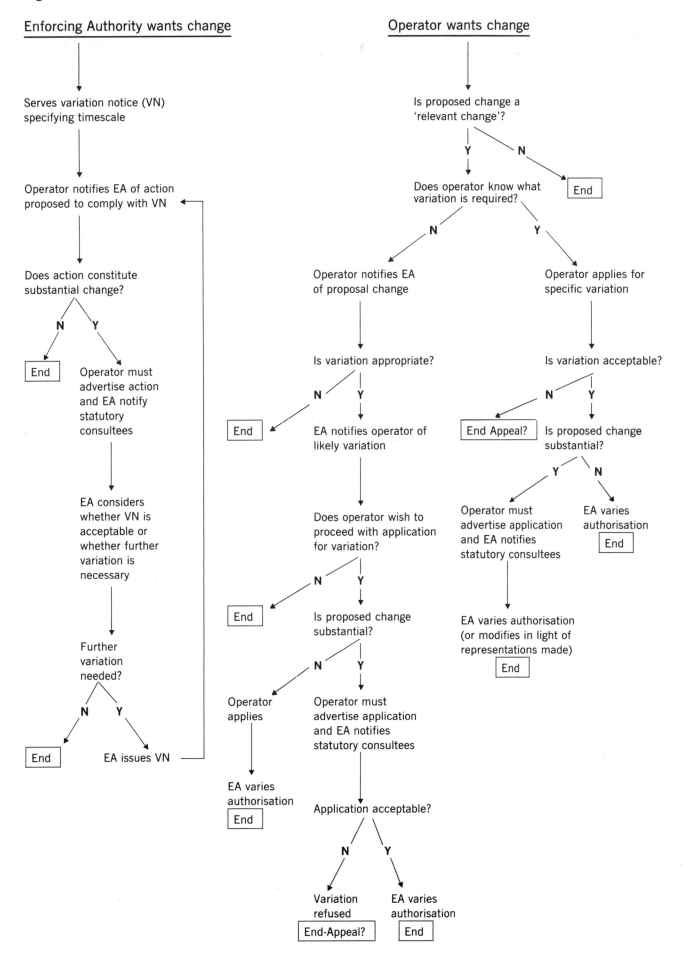

Enforcing Authority wants change

Serves variation notice (VN) specifying timescale

↓

Operator notifies EA of action proposed to comply with VN

↓

Does action constitute substantial change?

N → End

Y → Operator must advertise action and EA notify statutory consultees

↓

EA considers whether VN is acceptable or whether further variation is necessary

↓

Further variation needed?

N → End

Y → EA issues VN

Operator wants change

Is proposed change a 'relevant change'?

Y / N

N → End

Does operator know what variation is required?

N → Operator notifies EA of proposal change

Y → Operator applies for specific variation

Operator notifies EA of proposal change → Is variation appropriate?

N → End

Y → EA notifies operator of likely variation

↓

Does operator wish to proceed with application for variation?

N → End

Y → Is proposed change substantial?

N → Operator applies → EA varies authorisation → End

Y → Operator must advertise application and EA notifies statutory consultees

↓

Application acceptable?

N → Variation refused → End-Appeal?

Y → EA varies authorisation → End

Operator applies for specific variation → Is variation acceptable?

N → End Appeal?

Y → Is proposed change substantial?

Y → Operator must advertise application and EA notifies statutory consultees → EA varies authorisation (or modifies in light of representations made) → End

N → EA varies authorisation → End

Figure IV: Appeals – Written procedure

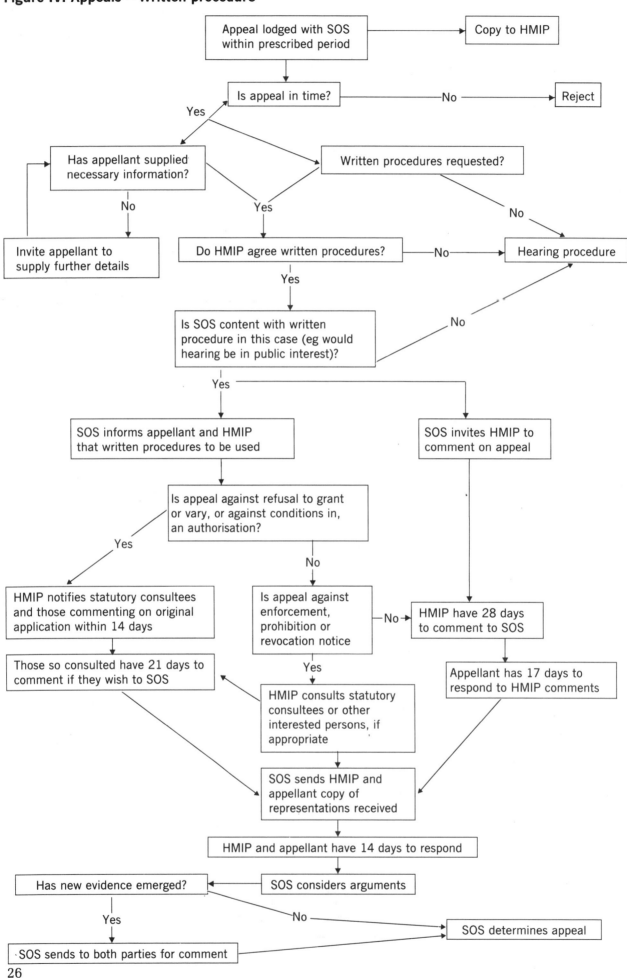

Timetable for implementing integrated pollution control

EPA Sched. 1 Ref	Process	Comes within IPC	Apply Between
	Fuel & Power Industry		
1.3	Combustion (>50MWth) Boilers and Furnaces	1.4.91	[1.4.91] & 30.4.91
1.1	Gasification	1.4.92	1.4.92 & 30.6.92
1.2	Carbonisation	1.4.92	1.4.92 & 30.6.92
1.3	Combustion (remainder)	1.4.92	1.4.92 & 30.6.92
1.4	Petroleum	1.4.92	1.4.92 & 30.6.92
	Waste Disposal Industry		
5.1	Incineration	1.8.92	1.8.92 & 31.10.92
5.2	Chemical Recovery	1.8.92	1.8.92 & 31.10.92
5.3	Waste Derived Fuel	1.8.92	1.8.92 & 31.10.92
	Mineral Industry		
3.1	Cement	1.12.92	1.12.92 & 28.2.93
3.2	Asbestos	1.12.92	1.12.92 & 28.2.93
3.3	Fibre	1.12.92	1.12.92 & 28.2.93
3.5	Glass	1.12.92	1.12.92 & 28.2.93
3.6	Ceramic	1.12.92	1.12.92 & 28.2.93

EPA Sched. 1 Ref	Process	Comes within IPC	Apply Between	Chief Inspector's Note Issues
Chemical Industry				
4.1	Petrochemical	1.5.93	1.5.93 & 31.7.93	1.11.92
4.2	Organic	1.5.93	1.5.93 & 31.7.93	1.11.92
4.7	Chemical Pesticide	1.5.93	1.5.93 & 31.7.93	1.11.92
4.8	Pharmaceutical	1.5.93	1.5.93 & 31.7.93	1.11.92
4.3	Acid Manufacturing	1.11.93	1.11.93 & 31.1.94	1.5.93
4.4	Halogen	1.11.93	1.11.93 & 31.1.94	1.5.93
4.6	Chemical Fertiliser	1.11.93	1.11.93 & 31.1.94	1.5.93
4.9	Bulk Chemical Storage	1.11.93	1.11.93 & 31.1.94	1.5.93
4.5	Inorganic Chemical	1.5.94	1.5.94 & 31.7.94	1.11.93
Metal Industry				
2.1	Iron and Steel	1.1.95	1.1.95 & 31.3.95	1.7.94
2.3	Smelting	1.1.95	1.1.95 & 31.3.95	1.7.94
2.2	Non-ferrous	1.5.95	1.5.95 & 31.7.95	1.11.94
Other Industry				
6.1	Paper Manufacturing	1.11.95	1.11.95 & 31.1.96	1.5.95
6.2	Di-isocyanate	1.11.95	1.11.95 & 31.1.96	1.5.95
6.3	Tar and Bitumen	1.11.95	1.11.95 & 31.1.96	1.5.95
6.4	Uranium	1.11.95	1.11.95 & 31.1.96	1.5.95
6.5	Coating	1.11.95	1.11.95 & 31.1.96	1.5.95
6.6	Coating Manufacturing	1.11.95	1.11.95 & 31.1.96	1.5.95
6.7	Timber	1.11.95	1.11.95 & 31.1.96	1.5.95
6.9	Animal and Plant Treatment	1.11.95	1.11.95 & 31.1.96	1.5.95

Prescribed Substances

Release to air:
Prescribed substances

Oxides of sulphur and other sulphur compounds
Oxides of nitrogen and other nitrogen compounds
Oxides of carbon
Organic compounds and partial oxidation products
Metals, metalloids and their compounds
Asbestos (suspended particulate matter and fibres), glass fibres and mineral fibres
Halogens and their compounds
Phosphorus and its compounds
Particulate matter.

Release to water:
Prescribed substances

Mercury and its compounds
Cadmium and its compounds
All isomers of hexachlorocyclohexane
All isomers of DDT
Pentachlorophenol and its compounds
Hexachlorobenzene
Hexachlorobutadiene
Aldrin
Dieldrin
Endrin
Polychlorinated Biphenyls
Dichlorvos
1,2-Dichloroethane
All isomers of Trichlorobenzene
Atrazine
Simazine
Tributyltin compounds
Triphenyltin compounds
Trifluralin
Fenitrothion
Azinphos-methyl
Malathion
Endosulfan.

Release to land:
Prescribed substances

Organic solvents
Azides
Halogens and their covalent compounds
Metal carbonyls
Organo-metallic compounds
Oxidising agents
Polychlorinated dibenzofuran and any congener thereof
Polychlorinated dibenzo-p-dioxin and any other congener thereof
Polyhalogenated biphenyls, terphenyls and naphthalenes
Phosphorus
Pesticides, that is to say, any chemical substance or preparation prepared or used for destroying any pest, including those used for protecting plants or wood or other plant products from harmful organisms; regulating the growth of plants; giving protection against harmful creatures; rendering such creatures harmless; controlling organisms with harmful or unwanted effects on water systems, buildings or other structures, or on manufactured products; or protecting animals against ectoparasites.
Alkali metals and their oxides and alkaline earth metals and their oxides.

HMIP offices and addresses

HMIP HEADQUARTERS

Romney House
43 Marsham Street
LONDON SW1P 3PY
Tel 071 276 8061
Fax 071 276 8605

HMIP NORTH DIVISION

Divisional Headquarters

Stockdale House (1st Floor)
Headingley Business Park
8 Victoria Road
Headingley
LEEDS LS6 1PF
Tel 0532 786636
Fax 0532 740464

North East Region

Stockdale House
LEEDS

Vincent House
2 Woodland Road
DARLINGTON DL3 7PJ
Tel 0325 380635
Fax 0325 467996

Don House
Pennine Centre
20–22 Hawley Street
SHEFFIELD S1 1HD
Tel 0742 700459
Fax 0742 762398

North West Region

Mitre House
Church Street
LANCASTER LA1 1BG
Tel 0524 302100
Fax 0524 382642

Unit 2
Kings Court
Manor Park
RUNCORN WA7 1HR
Tel 0928 579522
Fax 0928 579327

HMIP EAST DIVISION

Divisional Headquarters

Howard House
40–64 St John's Street
BEDFORD MK42 0DL
Tel 0234 272112
Fax 0234 218355

South Region

2 Marsham Street
LONDON SW1P 3EB
Tel 071 276 5594
Fax 071 276 6544

3 East Grinstead House
London Road
EAST GRINSTEAD
West Sussex RH10 1RR
Tel 0342 312016
Fax 0342 311565

Anglia Region

Howard House
BEDFORD

Mill House (4th Floor)
Brayford Side North
LINCOLN LN1 1YW
Tel 0522 512566
Fax 0522 546544

Carter House (4th Floor)
49–50 High Street
CHELMSFORD CM1 1DE
Tel 0245 490473
Fax 0245 495872

HMIP WEST DIVISION

Divisional Headquarters
Highwood Pavilions
Jupiter Road
Patchway
BRISTOL BS12 5SN
Tel 0272 794653
Fax 0272 794650

Midlands Region
McLaren Buildings
Room 1317
2 Masshouse Circus
Queensway
BIRMINGHAM B4 7NR
Tel 021 236 7674
Fax 021 236 1533

The Marches House
Midway
NEWCASTLE-UNDER-LYME
Staffordshire ST5 1DT
Tel 0782 711113

South West Region
Highwood Pavilions

Wales Region
Brunel House (11th Floor)
2 Fitzalan Road
CARDIFF CF2 1TT
Tel 0222 49558
Fax 0222 499924

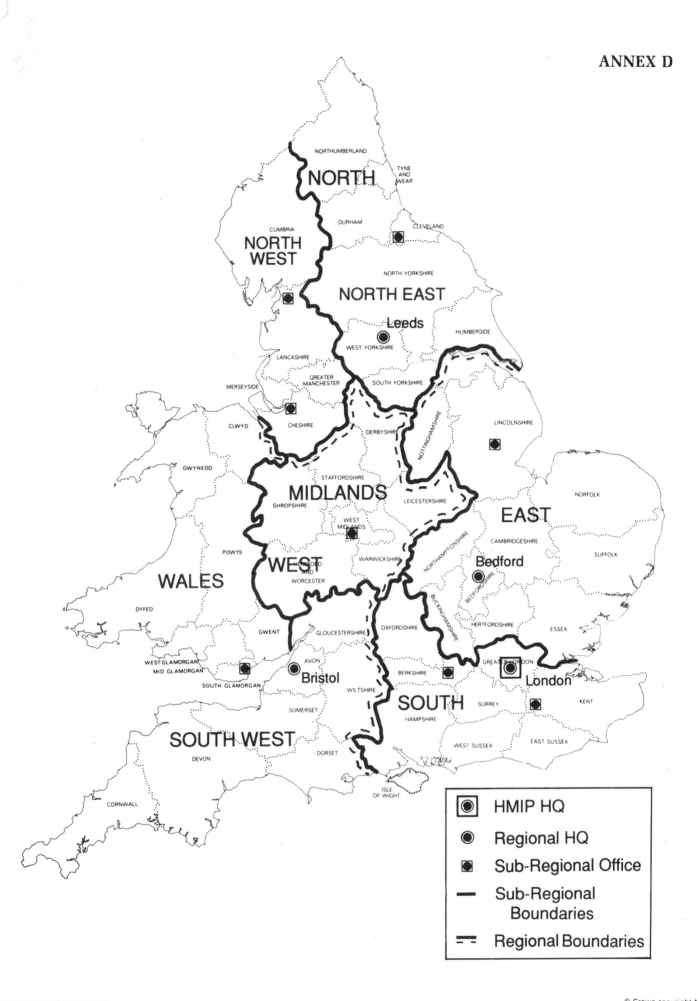

HMIP HQ

Regional HQ

Sub-Regional Office

— Sub-Regional Boundaries

-- Regional Boundaries

Mapping & Graphic Services OSD2